Exceptional Minds

Our mission is to maximize the talents
of artists on the autism spectrum with customized
instruction and hands-on experience to prepare
them for gainful work in digital arts and animation

Our vision is to empower people with autism to
achieve their full professional potential, and lead in
transforming global awareness of their capabilities.

www.Exceptional-Minds.org

First Edition
Published by Exceptional Minds Press
© 2019

ISBN: 978-0-578-22625-5

Comic idea by Jacob Lenard and Kate V Jorgensen
"ChickenHatGirl"
Book design by Jessica "Jess" Jerome
All contributions were made by
Exceptional Minds students and faculty.

See index for full list of illustrators.

This book is dedicated to all the creative artists at Exceptional Minds.

Special Thanks to Jacob and Kate "ChickenHatGirl", for coming up with the comic idea!

Special Thanks to Ryan for the book idea!

Exceptional Minds

Exceptional Minds is a professional training academy and studio for visual effects artists and animators with autism. We are a non-profit organization that transforms expectations through our mission of employability, self-sufficiency, and inclusion. Students at Exceptional Minds are artists who are learning how to express themselves and how to become gainfully employed. Every panel of this comic book was drawn by a different artist. Once someone drew a panel, they handed it off to the next artist to continue the story.

Enjoy "The Unpredictable Adventure of Jethro & Bork"!

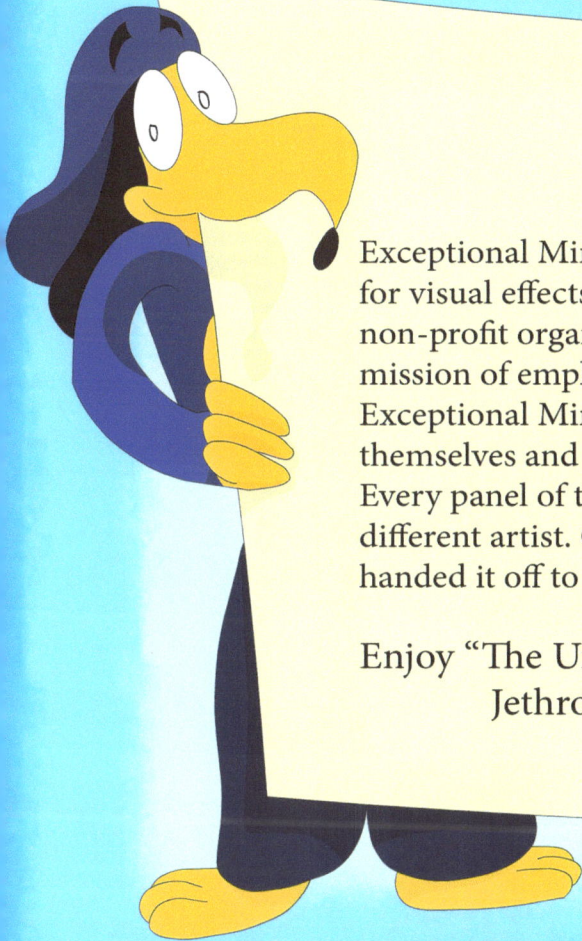

1. Jessica "Jess" Jerome

2. Dylan Carbonell

3. Michael A. Cicerelli

4. Sam O'Melia

5. S. Michael Hardin

6. Naseem Sabokpey

BEEP!

7. Max Everett

Kaboom

8. Zachary Warren

9. Dustin Noriyuki

10. Michael Shiu

11. Nick Dodge

Hey! those two blew up My brother bench!

12. Jacob Lenard

13. Sarah Barnes

14. Kate V Jorgensen "ChickenHatGirl"

15. Ryan Oldis

16. Tristan Maillet

17. Craig Hills

"Well, that's the last tune for a while, ladies & gentlemen."

18. Dustin Noriyuki

SLAM!

19. S. Michael Hardin

20. Zachary Warren

21. Sarah Barnes

22. Jacob Lenard

23. Nick Dodge

24. Michael Shiu

25. Craig Hills

26. Max Everett

27. Kate V Jorgensen "ChickenHatGirl"

28. Michael A. Cicerelli

29. Tristan Maillet

30. Sam O'Melia

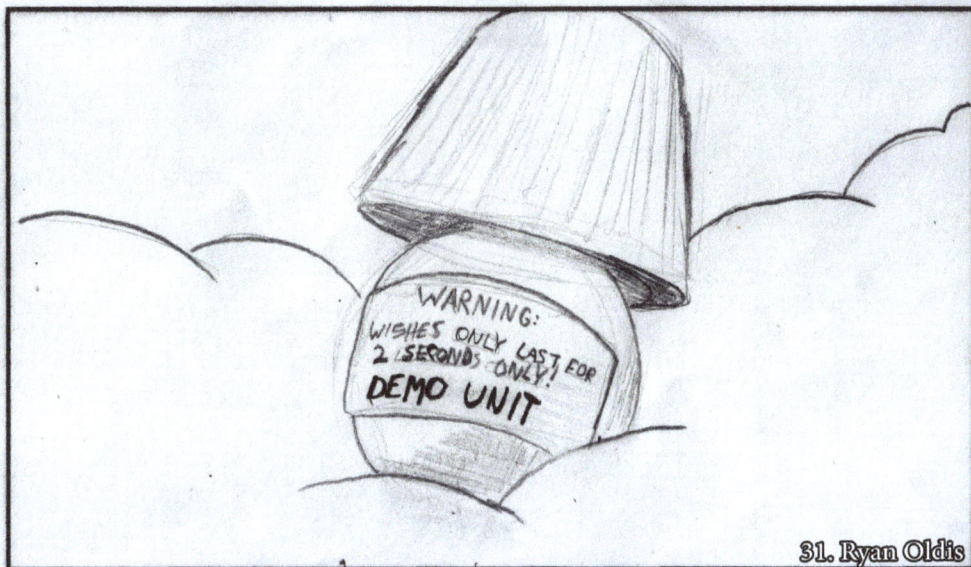
31. Ryan Oldis

32. Dylan Carbonell

33. Craig Hills

34. Naseem Sabokpey

35. Michael Shiu

SOMETHING IN THERE IS BOUND TO HELP US!

36. Z. William Payer

37. Mister Hayz

38. Jessica "Jess" Jerome

39. Jacob Lenard

40. Kate V Jorgensen "ChickenHatGirl"

what an unfortunate end.

the UNpREdicTable adventure of Jethro & Bork

Index

1. Jessica "Jess" Jerome*
2. Dylan Carbonell
3. Michael A. Cicerelli
4. Sam O'Melia
5. S. Michael Hardin
6. Naseem Sabokpey
7. Max Everett
8. Zachary Warren
9. Dustin Noriyuki
10. Michael Shiu
11. Nick Dodge
12. Jacob Lenard
13. Sarah Barnes
14. Kate V Jorgensen "ChickenHatGirl"
15. Ryan Oldis
16. Tristan Maillet
17. Craig Hills
18. Dustin Noriyuki
19. S. Michael Hardin
20. Zachary Warren
21. Sarah Barnes
22. Jacob Lenard
23. Nick Dodge
24. Michael Shiu
25. Craig Hills
26. Max Everett
27. Kate V Jorgensen "ChickenHatGirl"
28. Michael A. Cicerelli
29. Tristan Maillet
30. Sam O'Melia
31. Ryan Oldis
32. Dylan Carbonell
33. Craig Hills
34. Naseem Sabokpey
35. Michael Shiu
36. Z. William Payer*
37. Mister Hayz*
38. Jessica "Jess" Jerome*
39. Jacob Lenard
40. Kate V Jorgensen "ChickenHatGirl"

Faculty Members

www.ingramcontent.com/pod-product-compliance
Lightning Source LLC
Chambersburg PA
CBHW042012080426
42734CB00002B/58